CW00871355

To Jini & Liz
with best wishes
Christmas 2016.
Julie Wyness

Step by Slow Step

Rhoda Michael

Illustrated by Julie Wyness

Copyright © Rhoda Michael, 2016

The right of Rhoda Michael to be identified as the author
of this book has been asserted in accordance with the
Copyright, Designs & Patents Act 1988.
All rights reserved. No part of this publication may be reproduced,
stored in a retrieval system, or transmitted, in any form or by any means,
electronic, mechanical, photocopying, recording, or otherwise, without
the permission in writing from the publisher.

All illustrations Copyright © Julie Wyness

Design and typesetting: Leopard Press

Printed and bound in Scotland

A catalogue record for this book is available from the
Scottish National Library and the British Library

ISBN 978-0-9570999-7-5

Front Cover: Julie Wyness

STEP BY SLOW STEP

For the late Angus Dunn,
he really was the start for me

Contents

Editor's Note

I feel privileged to have Rhoda as a friend, having immense respect for her literary wisdom and am honoured to have been trusted with the role of editor of this project.

Perhaps Rhoda's finest achievement was to breathe new life into the Northwords Now magazine as a free newspaper. She joined the magazine in 2001 as poetry editor and went on to become editor in 2007. This was a tremendous task to which she brought intellectual rigour, enthusiasm and her enduring love of literature.

She chose what went into print, a responsibility which required reading hundreds of submissions to select a few. She was extremely generous with her time for those aspiring writers, including those she did not publish, by giving them constructive critiques of their work.

Thanks to the five years that she was editor, a swathe of writers had their first public platform and the publication she passed on when she retired in 2011 was a vibrant one, with national circulation.

All this time, and for many years before, she was writing her own short stories and poetry, contributing to many literary events, and regularly receiving recognition and awards for her work.

The value of her contribution in terms of supporting the endeavour of writers in Scotland, in nurturing new talent and in making a significant addition to the body of literary work, simply cannot be overestimated.

– Janet MacInnes

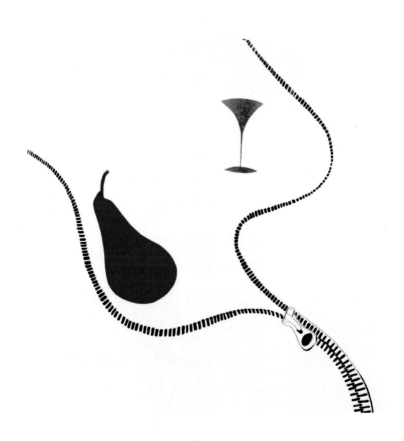

STEP BY SLOW STEP

Something Leather

Her message said she would be
wearing something leather.
Would like to meet, it said,
For company and fun, it said.
If things work out, go on maybe
to something further.

She'd be wearing something leather.
It would be red she said.
When she walked in, my head
told me I must be mad
to think that I could have
this gorgeous woman wearing her red leather.

I strode across the floor,
ordered whisky at the bar,
turned to her and asked her whether
I could get the same for her
or if she'd prefer,
I'd gladly offer something other.

She said she had a date.
I said, so then he's late,
does he expect that you will wait?
She said, he's not a mate,
he's just a guy gets in a state
over women wearing something leather.

I said why don't we dance a while?
I felt the promise in her smile.
She said, I like a man with style,
and when we left the bar, we left together.
She'd maybe go that extra mile, she said.
If I could zip her out of her red leather.

On a Shoulder of Canisp

July, and I am shy still
of this new love as he, I guess,
is not quite sure of me, of this
not quite as yet familiar love, in July
on this high shoulder of the hill.

The colours of the evening drift across
the undulations of the land.
From behind a slope below us
we see a sudden flush of hinds,
a herd, tight-bunched about with calves -
they stream fast-moving,
purposeful with thirst, towards the river
that curves beyond us out of sight.

They have dissolved themselves
into the land, hide into bracken,
hoof into tussock of grass. In the haze
of the evening, where we had seen them
all that's left is a quiver in the air.

This witnessing, it is a binding thing,
a clasping, a wedding of hands:
his to mine, mine to his,
on the high shoulder of the mountain
on this shy evening in July.

While the Balance of the Mind

It was always too late,
too late for us at the first time of telling.

'Not late at all,' they said,
'time still for choice,'
counting days into weeks,
computing
for the well-meant abortifacient.

But too late for us; you and I
joined by gut-cords, by whispers of
chemical shift in the cells, by blood-beat
already committed. No choice,
no days or weeks in our computation.

At term you are born
bare of the birth-gifts. Bud of your mouth
has no suck,
pink lark's tongue
has no song.
Pearly hand with perfect pink
lustre of nail has no curl
at the touch of my finger. Oh my darling,
of birth-gifts left bare.

No choice, no computation. For you
I stole. From your brother, your sister,
from your father - from them I stole,
leached nourishment out of the bread
of their lives, sapped their wine of its savour.

Unusable thefts, no suck,
no curl, no possible song. Thefts
unrestorable.

And now as it was
from the first time of telling,
no possible choice, no computation.
To this end we have come, that I make
for us now, my darling. Now
in the clear balance of my mind.

Audit

April evening, daylight still as I drive out.
I am invited to a country house. I wear
sleek silk. My car purrs with my achievement.

I feel a shock of property, beech trees
in plantation, budding in the evening haze;
green acreages promising return;
mallard, a couple, discussing prospects in wet grass;
pheasant strutting in secure possession
of the roads.

You hardly need slow down,
they judge their opportunity.
A stout one waddled, Provost, Godfather.
I still expected him to trot the last few steps.
The thuck on the bumper wasn't much.
In the rear-view mirror

he looms, lying in the road.
A kill! Exhilaration rushes high. So this
is why they hunt.
A ruby pool has spilt from his beak. Blood
would stain the pale upholstery of my car.
How then to gather my possession?

In the draught of a passing car one
dead wing flaps up. Sleek feathers
stroke my hand. I scream
and scream again
And stop, recover self-possession, re-
audit the account.

Gingerly

Gingerly, that's how I
flex my fingers,
that's how I probe my
crushed-up heart.

No broken bones then,
no visible bruising yet.
But the love I gave you
a total write-off;
in the wreckage
your voice an icy echo
'get out my way kid,
don't want you in my space.'

I didn't see it coming,
didn't read the road signs.
Thought you were my
one and only loving owner.
never guessed you were
a careless driver.
My insurance was
third party only.

So who will pay me
compensation?
Who would want to buy
a write-off broken heart?

Only Two Can Play

You told me we were playing a game
That only two could play.
I thought it would be you and me,
I never guessed you would betray.

I didn't know the rules of it,
I didn't understand.
I didn't know which cards to throw away,
Which ones to hold onto in my hand.

You were the one who dealt the cards,
You dealt out cards for three.
You let another player in,
The dummy, it was me.

You slipped her trump cards from your sleeve,
You let her take the winning trick.
She stole the tokens I had staked,
but it's you who was the cheat.

I thought that we were playing a game
That only two could play.
I never guessed that I would be
The one you would betray.

Snap

Snap of ice from the tray.
Snap again in the glass.
Ice-sharp sliver of sound,
slicing sound of the smile that I saw.
And the touch -

Your fingers
touching her lips. And her smile -
that was snap,
all snapped into place, the whispers,
the soft warning creaks in the ice.

And my tongue,
snap of tongue
hissing into your face.

Snap of ice in the glass,
cracking ice.

Snap of tongue,
get out now of my place.
Snap of ice
in the glass, cracking ice.

STEP BY SLOW STEP

In the Mirror

In the mirror, in the candle-light,
you could be anyone.

And in the winter, in the candlelight
anyone would do.

Missing Him

'Maudie', that's what he used to call to her,
'come into the garden, into the morning sun'.
And with her willow-pattern plate she'd go
down to the beds beyond the cypress hedge
where bees fussed among the clover-flowers
and butterflies, like sweet-pea petals, flitted through the
cabbages.

And he'd show her the treasures of the garden,
the dark quilting leaves of spinach, parsley
fronds of cress, and crimson radishes,
red lacquer blossoms on the tall bean canes.
He'd lift clumps of salads out for her
and lay them on the willow-pattern plate.

And sometimes, the way that he'd look at her,
she'd put the plate down deliberate
on the grass in the hot morning sun,
and he'd whisper, 'at our age, darling Maudie',
while the earth on the radishes
on the willow-pattern plate, warmed
to a soft dusty bloom.

Ansaphone

This is Tom Campbell speaking.
I can't take your call just now
but if you leave your name and number after the tone
I'll get back to you, **beep-beep-beep.**

'This is' - what a stupid thing
to put on an ansaphone. Do you
hear me Tom Campbell?
Of course you don't.
Because *'you'* is exactly what it isn't.

And you *'can't take my call'*?
I'm not 'giving' you a call.
That's not what this is; I
just wanted to speak - you remember 'speak'?
As in me saying, 'it's only me' and
you saying , 'it's yourself then' -
that's 'speak'.

And *'leave your name and number'*?
It's me, only me.
And if you need a name and number
don't bother with *'I'll get back to you...'*
because it's me, only me, speaking
after the **beep-beep-beep...**

Under a Covering of Leaves

We stir out of sleep. We cling
like lost children under a covering of leaves.
The knuckle of your thumb lies
wet against the corner of my mouth.
In the leaves of our sleep
I draw your knuckle in. Your mouth moves
damp against my forehead and you say
that I whimpered in the storm last night
when the tree went down in the lane.

The tree! We spring wide awake, tuck
pyjama legs into socks, button raincoats on
- chainsawed already, poor tree! Orange flesh
like one of those melons, and a dark hollow core.
Your legs quiver. I cling. The chainsaw men
want to take us home. Your eyes

go wide so they won't spill the tears.
The men fetch us their jackets and a flask of tea.
They show us how the ivy bit, soft mouths,
chains on chains of them. Clinging in.

When they've loaded up and gone
you run our hot bath - do you remember
our children playing together in the bath?
How absorbed they were,
trying to sink their wooden boats
that kept on and on bobbing up again.

When I try to speak about the ivy
your mouth moves warm against my forehead.
You were frightened, you say,
in the storm last night.
Until I whimpered, until you felt me cling.

Such a Sweet Liar

Sweetly you loved me, silver and honey, love,
tenderly lied to me, lying in your arms,
breath sweetly whispering silver endearments.
Tongue slowly filling my mouth with your honey.
Shouldn't have done it love, shouldn't have lied to me.
Such a sweet liar, love, lying in my arms.

Now you are lying on your pillow, love.
Claims of past wives and their children surround,
tenderly vying, outdoing, out-dying, love.
How should I hold you when such arms reach out to you.
Shouldn't have stolen my grief in the loss of you. Shouldn't
have crumpled my love in your hand.

Crack in the Plaster

She knows he has spoken:
small bones have crackled in her neck
and fog insulates her ear-drums.
From the wall above the hearth
a grain of plaster drops,
poises on the pile of the carpet.

Some days she finds
a small slag-heap of grains
trickling down one on another.
She used to store them in preserving jars,
thinking of the cost of restoration.

But now she has seen
where the last long split
will spring across the cornice
loosening
clumps of crumbling vine.

She has smelt sparked soot,
felt the draught that will flare
the cinders on the hearth,
heard the flames
that will power through the roof slates.

She has seen
how the chimney-stack will writhe,
how the rafters will splinter
into coals about his head.
She knows
that she will burn too.

Masks

- you know the ones. Theatres
put them on their playbills.
The mouth's the thing.
Look in the mirror,
try one on.

Lift the muscles back
across the cheek-bones -
that's a grimace yet:
a little further, good,
till you feel the skin press up around
the corners of the eyes.

There you have it,
the outside skin of merriment.
But it doesn't loosen
into full free play.
A knot of gristle
brakes it in
the dark well-bottom of the throat.

Try another one.

Draw down
the corners of the mouth behind
the upward outward push.
You feel it now, the face of grief?
In the roof-space of your mouth,
tongue in rigid thrust,
the unconnected clapper of a bell...

No need to practise tear drops.
Clowns
paint one on.

Solo

Coming up off the ferry
I drive into snow.
The familiar road now
sleeting ahead of me,
strung-out miles of it,
lurching cambers, sliding gradients,
a lonely way to go.

"You know I'll worry."
You'd said.
"Phone when you get there."
"I'll be thinking of you every minute,"
you'd said,
"all along the way."
So caring, that stuff

and me so grateful,
until I caught the drift.
You sitting comfortable,
I ploughing on solo,
up off the ferry ramp,
driving into snow.

Waiting for the Swallows

It's that time of year again
after all the winter rain
streaming down my window pane
and I'm waiting for the swallows.

It was our summer loving time
but then you left without a sign.
I didn't know which way you'd gone.
Now I'm here again alone
and waiting for the swallows.

Once we swooped from wire to wire
our wings a gleam of sapphire fire,
our heart-beats drumming our desire.
But then a storm-wind blew you higher.
I couldn't see, I couldn't follow.

It's that time of year again
after all the winter rain
streaming down my window pane
and I am waiting for the swallows.

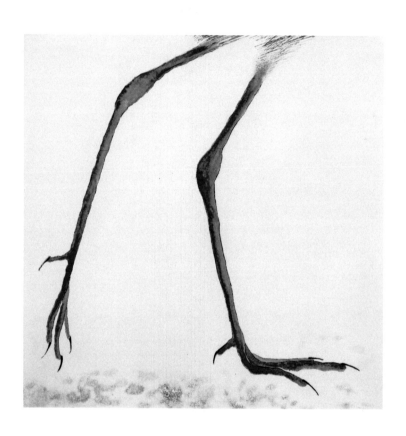

STEP BY SLOW STEP

Pi li li lui

The mist
lifts, and closes in, lifts
and closes in. Water
laps at the gravelled edge,
laps out, laps in. Pebbles
tumble one half turn and roll
in long connected threads,
roll running faster out
then slow again, steady
in the lapping turn.

The bird's red feet
step searching through the flow
that streams between the pebbles.
The bird mews, and mews again,
searching the mist along the shore.

She waits in the rhythms of the turning day.
Neighbours come and the postman
and the travelling van. She waits
counting nothing,
nothing forward,
nothing back. Footsteps draw up close,
voices say her name.
The voices and the footsteps
die away.

The mist lifts and the bird
cries clearer now, *pi li li lui,*
harsh along the edge. Water laps,
shells shift, click-tip, pebbles strung
on long connected threads roll-shrush,
and the thrum of the van and
the rush of the feet meet
the cry of the bird, *pi li li liu,* sharp
along the endless sky.

In pre-Christian Celtic myth the redshank searches for the souls of the
dying to guide them beyond the worlds of earth, air and water.
In an ancient Celtic lament *pilililiu* is an attempt to imitate the red-
shank's flight-cry.

Nest

She'd filled the basket with primroses,
damp-rooted, tucked around with moss.
Not much of a one for kissing, she
handed them up to me at the last moment
before the train drew out.

When I unpacked the primroses
six buff pullets' eggs
nestled in the moss.

Back Lane

- full daze of sunlight there, a vista
down the line of lock-up garages.
Dust-painted doors define themselves
as cobalt, crimson lake, viridian.
Blue lupin strands revert to lavender
and mimulus, profusely orange,
jungles, succulent,
below a dripping rone.

Spring Morning

Two hours below us on the thaw-flooded
grasses of the riverbank it is already Spring.

We have grunted, a trail of us, knitted up,
strung out over roots of rock and heather
between the man ahead of us, compass
on his wrist, map case round his neck,
and the pair at the back, tyrants
behind whom we are not allowed to straggle.

We breast the last long sudden steep
out onto the high plateau. Thaw-mist drifts
thin above wet snow. Our boots go in knee-deep.

Lilac Tree

Soft lilac sandstone village
soft light in the evening lane
high lilac sound in the evening's whispering
when the child must cross the lane.

Pale silent sandstone village
pale light in the evening lane
sharp high scent of the lilac singing
above a descant of switching pain.

Frayed switch in the lilac evening
frayed lilac beads on the skin
frayed high sound in the evening whispering
when the child has crossed the lane.

Peewit

Vee-veet, she nags at them,
flighting low along
the puddled gravel of the road.
Four, five delinquent little puffs of things
tipsying on rosy high-heeled toes,
they'll go on giggling till she's got them all in bed.

There's not a gap for them for miles.
Two handfuls twice and I'd have
put them in the field -
vee-veet, vee-vee-vee-veet,
a hundred peewits circle.

When I look down again,
a line of gold-flecked agates
is set in the gravel of the road.

Zebra Day

Air hangs grey beneath the trees.
A seagull glides white into view,
dips one wing and curves away again.
Shoes crunch on gravel and voices,
light as pebbles pinking over scree slopes,
ask the way to the penguins.

Then, up ahead, uniforms, jerseys
with elbow-patches, green peaked hats:
keepers, five or six of them,
hands flat-palmed against a high-wired fence,
faces focused in, like fathers
at a junior-school football match.

A zebra is rolling in the sparse grey grass.
Dust rises and the stocky striped legs
stretch and flex in the air. She's galloping
across a shimmering plain. She's racing
through hot white shadows. She
clambers up, heavy-muscled in the thighs.

Broad neck arches down to a folded
handful of stripes that she nudges onto legs
nudges into movement till it finds her flank
and mumbles at the taut dark udder.

The keepers look away, push peaked hats
back off their foreheads, scratch at thinning hair,
rustle loose change in their pockets.
A blink of sunshine breaks through the grey
and stripes their shy bright faces.

Mosquito

Arctic air-base jet fighter plane, the first
mosquito-whine subliminal blasts up the
decibels, roars down the frequencies,
breath-stopping vacuum in the lung-cage. The next
a slug of high-grade octane in the bloodstream,
you dare not raise your eyes to look at them.
They'll dazzle you to blindness. The third one
swirls you round while you're still reeling.

Above the snow-pools of the tundra, the mouth parts
of the female swoop strike sting mosquito
in the brief hormonal daylight pierce
and siphon off your blood.

Little Girl

Little tumbling girl, tumbled into sleep
before you could wash her,
little plum
with that perfect bloom.

If she was a kitten you could
lick her face clean till
she purred and you
purred and purred.

Girl Inside

Here's a new girl coming
but there's no great iron clang,
just an electronic hiss,
no preparation that for the life inside.
Let's ask her what she's in for.
She doesn't hear us. She's staring,
staring at something inside her head.
Shaved head. Hygienic that, in here;
and in fights no handfuls to drag you down.
Big disadvantage though,
can't hide your face. The look on it,
bit of temper there, bit of stubbornness.
Never blossomed, that face,
nipped by frost early on.
D'you think she knows what it's like
locked up alone, hour after hour,
counting each minute of the electronic clock
till you want to have bars you can rattle,
not that complacent wall.
Listen to her, grinding her teeth, and moaning,
like the wind in an empty drain.
She's cutting into her arms with her nails.
Scars there too, must have done that before.
Must have cut deep, must have felt real bad
to cut that deep. And now she's stabbing.
And stabbing. If she had a knife, but …

Paeony Roses

You hear the faintest moment of silence,
of him not being the breath and the sound
that you hear, just that moment
of sound not being there

and you move -

Hah! He's there,
over there at the paeony roses
reaching up and pulling the petals,
trying to catch at
the little white flutter
that falls through his outspread fingers.

You call and he turns,
you gather up the petals,
hold his sticky hands flat,
trickle down a shower on his open palms,

and he laughs, plunging for more
but you hold him back, show him
how to breathe in the scent,
breathe it deep from the flower.

You lift him up,
and you breathe the scent together, you
heady with the feel of him, he
sounding like the grunt of
this-little-piggy-ran all-the-way-home.

idreamtihadahad

I dreamt I had a dad
coming down the street he was
coming down to me.
I dreamt I had a dad, I did
I dreamt I had a dad.

I could see him searching
in all the cardboard boxes
and all the people shouting
do not open up our boxes
do not touch our boxes, don't.
I dreamt I had a dad.

And in my dream I shouted
Listen to the music, dad
when you open up the lid of it.
Listen to the music
coming from my box.

I dreamt
I heard my daddy say
when you coming home son?
You know your mammy missing you.
That's what I heard my daddy say.

When you coming home son?
You know your mammy missing you.
I dreamt I had a dad, I did
Listening to my music box.
I dreamt I had a dad.

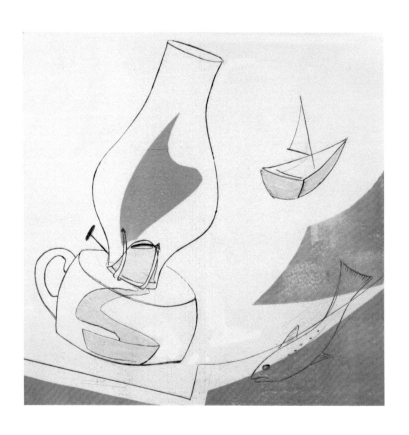

Bearings

My grandparents' house has a window
built up into the roof, high and wide
with a full view over the Sound.
That's where my grandmother watched
for my grandfather's boat coming in.
And in the childhood years that I lived there
she would let me go up to watch with her.

In winter, darkness would fall before he got in
and she would light the oil-lamps on the shelf.
He told me that was the light he looked for
to give him his bearing in.

I still have the lamps and I've refurbished them
back into working order. When I light them,
the sweet smell of oil fills the house with a memory
of voices and the taste of my grandmother's scones.

I hardly remember my mother,
just a fragrance of roses that comes to me sometimes
and a faint sensation of silk.

Hallow's Eve

This is the night of dead souls, of lantern shadows
and ducking for apples,
down to the living rose of their skin,
and laughing and pushing
down through the water to reach the faces
of drowned men, down drowned,
sliding down.

He pedals his tricycle out,
little tricycle out on a filling wave
till he sees his father's face and his hands
pushing up in the rolling glass - so near.
So near.

He dips down, down, so far,
and the face
breaks into ripples; in his hand
only dripping salt.

The water-witch laughs, blowing green salt bubbles.
You're too young, little boy, only three,
to pedal through salt green glass.
No!
I'm nearly four. I can reach, I nearly can.

The tricycle skids down the switchback slide
of the salt green glass. Sweeps him down.
There's the face again. He pedals, pedals, knees
huge to his chin in grown man's trousers.
Hold on!
Daddy, hold on!

The face
breaks into salt green ripples. It is gone
Gone.
He is gone.

The grown man wakes, face
drenched with joy,
drenched with fresh salt tears.
In the night his drowned father came.
In the night
his drowned father kissed him.

Conscripted

They came for us early in the day,
marked us off against their lists,
pushed us to our places in the column.
Near me, now, is no-one that I knew.

We have marched this far.
We're coming closer now
to the shadow in the wall
through which each steps
and is hidden.

It was after the rain that I shivered,
that I longed for my jacket
in the bag we may not open.

My mother's fingertips this morning
pressed each stitched cushion
of the quilting of the jacket. She pressed
her mouth against my ear,
'Remember nothing.
And on those nights when
the moonlight sobs
especially then, long for nothing.'

The crush of her hand
has raised a callus in my palm.
Her dry hard kiss becomes
the stone she has embedded in my forehead.

Mirrored

That's it then, best to look it in the face.
It's gone beyond tears,
See, the eyes quite dry.
I've washed my hair clean of the ashes,
Put off the sackcloth, dressed my body in soft clothes.
Now grief will not stare back at me
From other people's gaze.

I'm an ordinary woman,
but now I know the meaning
of extraordinary words.

Rachel weeping for her children,
Would not be comforted
Because they are not.

Not Lightly Packed

It was the neat way you tied the buckles
that made me call you back.
'He's going to run away', you said,
your face crumpled with the weight of it.
I knew you meant your little brother.

It was hours before I brought myself
to pick the rucksack up.
You'd packed clean socks
and one of those soft-leaved lettuces.

You'd folded the socks one inside the other,
I didn't know you could.
And you'd tried to wash the lettuce. You
had not lightly packed.

Gibbous Moon

Her world has contracted
to the view from her window
when she lies propped on her pillows.
Across the months she watches
the passage of the moon, its appearances,
recognises its waxing and its wane.
She looks forward to its fullness;
is tender towards the first thin sliver
of each new one.
Envies it the predictable period
of its ending;
envies the gibbous moon.

STEP BY SLOW STEP

Winter Garden

Damp silence hangs beneath the trees.
In the turned soil
only the gnarled stems of cabbages
and drab tangles of grass.

Footsteps crunch on the gravel of the path.
You'd think our father was the sun
the way the light round us changes;
and when he asks if we remember apples
my teeth bite into greenness
and my tongue tastes sparkles of gold.

Look up to the top of the tree, he says.
And we do,
up through the bare black branches.
Electric fast the first apple gleams
and again and again the gleam
till we each hold one in our hand.

Do more, we urge, more more,
jumping in our brown laced shoes.
But his arms on our shoulders hold us
and we know his strength when he tells us
of the gladness of just enough.

Good Cup of Tea

He sips from the cup the nurse is holding.
It's hot and clean with that first fresh release of tannin.
He sips again and then again,
then that flicker in the muscles of his arms,
he wants to hold the cup himself.
The nurse pushes extra pillows in,
puts the cup in his two hands.
It's wonderful, holding it like that,
it stirs something on the edge of memory,
somethings that makes his hand shake.
He can see the tea slop in little waves,
he's afraid that if it spills he'll cry.
But it doesn't spill.
'Another sip?' she asks. He's forgotten she is there.
He drinks mouthfuls.
He can hear himself guzzle,
like a calf, somewhere a long time ago,
a calf guzzling draughts from a bucket,
and voices, in sunlight, laughing.

'You were thirsty', the nurse laughs softly.
He tries his voice, he can manage it,
'Good cup of tea'.

Piano

His feet shuffle. His lungs seize in the frozen air.
He's foraged nothing, nothing that will burn.
Elyena stares up at him from the pillows of their bed.
He takes the axe from his belt. Slams it down.
The first stroke glances off
the hard polished wood of the piano.
Elyena tries to rise, screaming at him not to damage it.
He slams again, splinters loosening,
the big iron frame of the piano booming,
mad chords jangling from the wires,
the performance of his life.
At their door, hammering, neighbours
from other rooms, just like them, frozen, starving.
The men bring their axes, more clashing chords,
more iron clangour.
                    When all that dies away
from somewhere over to the west
they hear the guns again. How quiet now,
like party pop-guns. They cram the stove,
they orgy, all of them, all night, on fire.

News

Science News

Brain-stems (of women)
during pregnancy
shrink.
Recovery (of size)
takes time.

Local News

Two cars collided
and went, as can happen,
on fire. Firemen
released the drivers but
could not reach
a baby
in a cot.

National News

The mother
(brain-stem shrunk...) saw only
the child
in the cot
in the flames
through which
(though the firemen, distraught, did try to stop her)
she leapt,
reaching the cot but
dying
several days later
of burns

Local News

The child (the cot was of fire-retardant material)
lives, relatively (as far as can be scientifically measured)
unscarred.

Science News

Brain-stems ...

It wasn't Her

I'm so affronted. Her next door,
it's her that phoned the Social.
That child's off her head, attacked me,
raked my arm with her nails, see?
She's nine now, she's strong.
All I did was send her to her room
but she grabbed her presents. And the cake,
that cake that I made her.

So, I'm exhausted.
I turn the key in her door, that's all I do.
The next I know it's the doorbell ringing.
And ringing.
I don't want to answer but I have to.
And that's when I see,
the presents, the cake all smashed up.
Splat! Down there among the begonias.

It wasn't funny, the damage, every flower head off.
And the shouting!
Talk about tell it from the roof-tops,
the things I was supposed to have done to her.
The humiliation!
And her next door watching everything,
a social worker, in this house. And two police.

She wouldn't speak to them, no need now was there.
Got me where she wanted me - and the questions,
I'm the one who had to answer the questions.
Right of silence? What right of silence?
She's the one who had that.
Missing her father? I told them the truth -
missing the spoiling, more like, when he was here,
when he could be bothered.

Yes, I said, she could see him.
If we had an address. If he'd even sent a card.
Four years now
And not a penny, not a single word.
And the worst is, she doesn't seem to realise
It wasn't her he left.

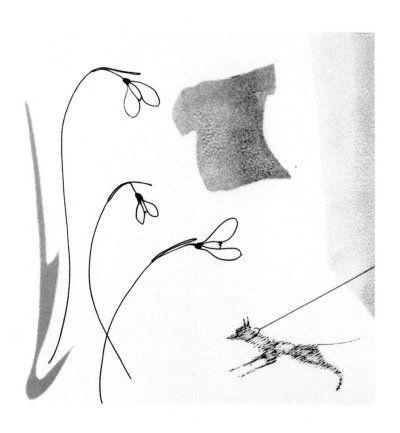

STEP BY SLOW STEP

Detritus Dancing

Closed stone Sunday tenements,
streets bleached bone-dry,
dead-ice smell in the wind.

Then a glimpse,
in the angle of a granite wall,
white snowdrops
which, on a spiral gust,
eddy upwards,
transfigured
to a crumpled paper bag
which arcs
across the bone-dry street
and dances
over bleached straw grass
till a young dog tugging for play
dances after it.

High on a granite wall
a window opens.
A pink shirt billows and a voice
parachutes down
to the boy who is tugged by the dog
'Wait for me, wait for me'

Sleight-of-hand

We have tickets for the circus.
Their honking drum-roll orchestra
puts us in the mood. We hold our breath
with terror for the acrobats,
are dazzled by the jugglers flashing skill.
We laugh like children with the clowns,
at dogs in frilly skirts, at dancing bears.

They bring on a troupe of cats.
They are domestic cats, a mixed lot,
of stripes, black and white, ginger mottle,
ordinary indignant household pets.
These cats perform like acrobats.
They swing through sets of swinging ladders,
they somersault on parallel bars.

We are slow to realise the brilliance
of the sleight-of-hand, to see
that it's not that the cats have learned tricks;
it's the jugglers who make it seem like that.
They bow when we applaud the wit
of their performance, when they see
that their effrontery delights.

Last Things

Floor-boards creak already,
wood easing itself
now the weight of the furniture is gone.
Shifts in the air disperse old fragrances -
ironed tablecloths
storing a memory of freshness;
orange peel on the fire, Christmases
upon Christmases.

They've left that flower-pot on the windowsill.
All that singing and laughing, all that playing
with the bright bouncing ball till it fell -
red chips of clay, damp scattering of soil.
Between finger and thumb
dead stems crumble like thin rusted wire
releasing
the last dry breath of geranium.

STEP BY SLOW STEP

Pussy-cat, Pussy-cat

Amadeus, the cat, slides through the dew
of a soft savannah, thigh muscles slick
as a violin bow, hair tips stroking the grass.

Through slits in his eyes' green walls he watches
the movement of air on the play of the stems.
Something new moves. Paw strikes.
Cat waits, desire sustained, watching
for the grass-stir that triggers
the next ramping strike. Smug play of paw.

He can play like this, who knows how long,
linked strings of structured pleasure,
ripped threads of stretching pain.

He saunters back to the house at last, flows
knowingly around my ankle bones, slides
haunches down, front paws possessive
across the pale kid slippers on my feet.

Full Flags

I have come to make camp in a strange country.
I have folded down my flags. I have pared myself
to an essential point. This silent hurtled head,
this scoured flesh: I am his father. This
is my injured child.

They treat me with a strange courtesy,
they who come and go about his bed. I want
to cleave him to my bones. I risk a half-breathed kiss
on his bruised skin. A pitched sigh escapes. I flinch
from his unconscious pain.

I damp down fires. Mind focuses all energy to keep
the watches of the camp.
A tongue of flame breaks through my guard,
the need to bargain, to make promises. I steal
along the silent hum of the night-corridor to find
a place to pray. Arranged flowers flank a tactful crucifix. I feel
the pierce of wounded flesh, race back
along the corridor.
In the strange country where my pierced son lies
he is still courteously, still watchfully, attended.

His mother comes. Old angers stir.
But for this moment, for this child of our once love
she too folds down her flags.
Primitive juices flow, the surge to seed myself. She too.
We snatch ourselves apart.
We seek humility. We submit our will
to mend this child.

Days, weeks go by. Eyes open.
A smile of recognition. Speech comes back.

They have drawn a map for us with mountain passes
and pathways through the marshes marked. The journey
will be long, but for today -

today, I am allowed to bring him home. We may
strike camp. We may ride out together from this courteous place.

We ride with silver bells on prancing horses.
We present, my precious mending son and I,
to the wide world our scarlet pennons,
our full flags flying in the laughing wind.

Step by Slow Step

Icon

We've done the jewelled artefacts, sarcophagi
carved from single lumps of malachite, gilded sledges
for imperial journeys through the snow.
We've trailed round mediaeval monasteries,
stared at italianate interiors, surfeited
on schools of painting and their dates.

I long for my fireside chair at home
and a good spy story or a glossy magazine.
But even now, on this last day,
on our jaded senses, another gallery,
further images, one more icon, to be imposed.

We realise the status of this object
from the armed and guarded space around.
The guide maps this icon's history, its place
through the events of centuries;
at times of public terror, in hours of private need.

She draws our gaze to the Madonna's face,
speaks of the foreknowledge in her eyes, and
despite what is foreknown, the gentle giving visible
in this holy mother's hands.

It's only wood, I tell myself, and clever paint.
Then nip back tears. For several moments
we all respect each others' privacy.

Then someone says, so that's an icon then.
And someone nods.

Imprints

You know they're in there,
the layered landscapes,
slide open any drawer;
map on map of them,
relief lines flattened,
out of recognition,
leached pastels shifting,
in the slippy air.

What's that squirm there? Slide
the drawer back softly,
let the magnets of
the runners draw it in.
Dust particles develop colour, cluster
- slam it tight!

A claw-tip catches, something dribbles.
Now that drawer won't shut.

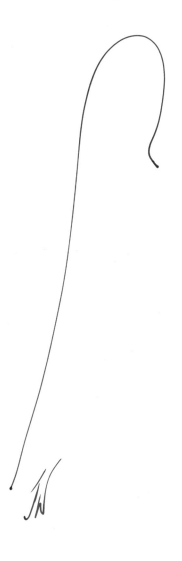

STEP BY SLOW STEP

SONGS OF ISHMAEL:

My name is Ishmael

My name is Ishmael. I am Abraham's only son.
I know this to be true from the way he lays
his hand upon my head. This is known
to all who live within my father's tents.
But in the play fields, when I say my father's name,
I've seen smirks behind their hands
on some boys' faces. I tried once
to ask my father why this happened,

but his hand pressed my head against
the hollow of his belly and his eyes
looked away. I will not ask him this again.
But when I'm older, when my arms are stronger,
I'll twist the meaning of it out of them,
I'll wipe the smirking off their furtive faces.

Hagar

Hagar is my mother. She has been my father's wife
but he has given her no tent. She has no people,
nothing that belongs to her. My father's lawful wife
is Sarah, and it's in the shadows of the tents
of Sarah that my mother has to live. She is the least

of Sarah's handmaids. She must attend to Sarah's feet
which smell. Skin suppurates and toenails thicken
like the horns of rancid goats. My mother's hands
are careful as she cleanses, pares the nails,
dresses Sarah's feet with scented oils.

I've seen Sarah push my mother off
the carpets of the tent with her wet feet,
call her maids to scrub my mother's hands
in dry sand, scour raw the scented layers
off her skin. Makes them press in salt -

When my mother pleads
Sarah laughs. I crush
my knees into my belly, bind
my arms about my head.

They do these things to my mother
only when my father
is travelling with his flocks.

The Flocks Come Home

Across the summer Abraham has travelled with his flocks.
The sheep are fat, they have multiplied. And now he brings them home.
The young men run ahead of him to tell of his approach.
Cooking fires glow red upon the hearthstones. Lambs dressed with oil
and fragrant herbs are roasting. Women sway to the rhythm
of the kneading of the bread. Cups of wine flow over.
Shepherds with their pipes announce him. He laughs as the maidens
of the cisterns slide off his weary garments, draw him to be bathed.
They sing as they comb the tangles from his beard, anoint him,
dress him in a robe new woven from the fleece of this year's lambs.

They lead him to sit with Sarah on the carpets of his tent.
She sits at his right hand: she is his lawful wife. She
offers him the choicest morsels of the feast, pours him wine.
Shepherds, freshly bathed and robed sit with them. Singers
sing their praises. Tales are told of their adventures.
Hagar stands among Sarah's servants: her hand on my shoulder.
Abraham glances across at us. His smile flickers. He nods.
My mother's grip tightens. I am invited forwards.
I may place my hands upon his knees.
He calls me Ishmael. He lays his hands on my head.

Figs

As I doze
in the heat and the silence
of the slow afternoon
I see my father enter at
the curtain of the tent.

My mother springs awake,
her eyes flare. His upraised palms
plead thirst. My mother thrusts
our bowl of figs against his breast.
Their eyes hold. His hand

gropes blind to find the fruit.
Thumbnails split the purple skin, press
the oozing to my mother's mouth.
He lays the empty fig-skin in the bowl,
offers his fingers to her tongue.

She sucks the drowsy honey
slowly, off each finger, one by one.

When I wake again he has gone.

God's Promise

Abraham, in his secret heart rejoices. He has
God's promise, he is to have a lawful son.
He is rich, his flocks have multiplied.
He will have a son who can inherit,
from him kings and nations are to spring.

For Ishmael, whose ringlets spring
beneath the hand like young lambs skipping,
Abraham's heart is troubled. He knows the heat
that burns in him. He knows that he will sacrifice
the heart of Ishmael to get himself a lawful son.

Covenant

Today is the day of circumcision,
of sacred covenant. Kings and nations
are to spring from my father's seed.
They will inherit, they will flourish.

My father, Abraham, is old. His skin
hangs slack in wrinkles from his belly.
I am my father's only son.
                              Today
I may drink wine from my father's cup.
I am thirteen years old.
                         It is the day
Of circumcision which will be the sign,
down through the generations, of God's promise.
My father Abraham is old. I am his only son.
I am to walk beside him to the sacrament
I walk with him in the brightness of the day.

False Promise

Across the months of this year's grazing,
when my father's flocks go travelling,
in my father's place I am to lead them.

He has given me my own tent and servants
to attend me, has placed the master
of his shepherds under my command.

We shall spread our tents by leisured pastures.
Our flocks will crop on green crammed grasses,
they will stroll among their lambs in easy folds.

And in the courtyards of the fountains,
when moonlight sparkles on the waters,
when the maidens of the fountains dance among us,

we shall hear the trickled music of
their silver tambourines. All these things
my father has arranged for me
across the months of this year's grazing
when I travel in his place to lead his flocks.

Nativity

Across the months the flocks have multiplied
and now, today, Ishmael leads them home.
Cold light cuts the east horizon.
Shepherds push off sleep. They shiver.
Ishmael runs on ahead of them. He longs
to have his father's blessing. He yearns
to feel his father's hands upon his head.

His father's tents are sharp black shadows
against the flaring of the morning sun.
His father's people are squat dark shadows.
Crouched in silence they wait, expectant.
Surely it's him they wait for. Ishmael runs.
His joy flows over. His father steps out from
the curtain of his tent. Ishmael

falls forward on the ground before him,
awaits the touch of raising hands. His father's voice
commands attention. Ishmael hears
a stir of joyful murmur. He lifts his head.
His father's hands hold out a swaddled bundle
which he presents to his assembled people.
'Behold', Abraham's voice rejoices.

'Behold him whose name is Isaac,
who shall be my first-born son'.